GREATEST WARRIORS
GREEK SOLDIERS

ALEX STEWART

ARCTURUS

This edition first published in 2014 by Arcturus Publishing

Distributed by Black Rabbit Books
P.O. Box 3263
Mankato
Minnesota MN 56002

Edited and designed by: Discovery Books Ltd.

Library of Congress Cataloging-in-Publication Data

Stewart, Alex, 1950-
 Greek soldiers / Alex Stewart.
     pages cm. -- (Greatest warriors)
 Includes index.
 Summary: "Provides readers with exciting details, facts, and statistics about historical Greek soldiers"--Provided by publisher.
 Audience: Grades 4-6.
 ISBN 978-1-78212-399-6 (library binding)
 1. Military art and science--Greece--History--To 1500--Juvenile literature. 2. Soldiers--Greece--History--To 1500--Juvenile literature.
 3. Greece--History, Military--To 146 B.C.--Juvenile literature. I. Title.
 U33.S74 2013
 355.00938--dc23
                           2013005689

Series concept: Joe Harris
Managing editor for Discovery Books: Laura Durman
Editor: Clare Collinson
Picture researcher: Clare Collinson
Designer: Ian Winton

The publisher would like to thank Koryvantes.org for their assistance in the preparation of this book.

Picture credits:
Alamy: pp. 7, 18, 23, 27 (AF archive), p. 20 (Moviestore collection Ltd), p. 24 (National Geographic Image Collection), p. 25 (Maurice Crooks); Getty Images: p. 19 (Time & Life Pictures), p. 22 (AFP); Koryvantes.org: pp. 4, 5r, 9, 10, 11, 14b, 15, 17, pp. title, 6t, 8, 12, 13, 14t (armor research/reconstruction by Hellenicarmors.gr), p. 16 (re-enactment of Marathon battle by various international hoplite groups), p. 21t (courtesy of Spathia.com, research/reconstruction by Dimitrios Tertsis); Shutterstock Images: p. 5l (Ivan Montero Martinez), p. 6b (Kardmar), p. 26 (Yiannis Papadimitriou); Wikimedia Commons p. 21b (Ron L. Toms).
Cover images: Koryvantes.org: top, bottom centre (armor research/reconstruction by Hellenicarmors.gr); Shutterstock: background (Anastasios71).

Printed in China

SL002665US
Supplier 03, Date 0513, Print Run 2356

CONTENTS

GREECE AT WAR

In ancient Greece, every free man was a warrior. Greece was made up of hundreds of mini countries known as **city states**, and every city state had an army. The most powerful city states were Athens and Sparta.

A UNITED FORCE
Greek warriors from different city states joined together to fight off foreign invaders. They developed **tactics** and weapons that made them the premiere fighting force of their day.

TERRIFYING IMAGES
Greek warriors carried heavy spears, and shields painted with frightening images to scare their enemies.

ATHENS VS. SPARTA

The city states of Greece sometimes united against a common enemy. They also fought among themselves in bitter battles. Athens and Sparta were the deadliest enemies. Their rivalry boiled over into the long and bloody **Peloponnesian War (431–404 BCE).**

DEADLY SPARTAN

Spartan warriors were the fiercest soldiers in Greece. One Spartan, the saying went, was worth several soldiers from any other city state.

LAMBDA

Spartan shields were often decorated with the Greek letter "lambda." This stood for Lacedaemon, the ancient Greek name for the region of Sparta.

COMBAT STATS

The Peloponnesian War, 431–404 BCE

- **Fought between:** Athens and its allies vs. Sparta and its allies
- **Sparta's greatest strength:** the toughest army in Greece, with 6,000 **professional** soldiers
- **Athens' greatest strength:** a huge navy of 400 ships and 80,000 sailors
- **Turning point:** Athenian force of 200 ships and 10,000 troops wiped out by Sparta in Sicily, 415–413 BCE
- **Outcome:** unconditional surrender by Athens after 27 years of fierce fighting
- **Casualties:** an average of 123 deaths per day

WARRIOR KINGS

Long before the Peloponnesian War, during the period 1600–1100 BCE, Greece was dominated by the Mycenaeans. The Mycenaeans were ruled by powerful warrior kings. They fought with **bronze** weapons and lived in military strongholds, protected by massive stone walls.

BRONZE ARMOR
The Mycenaeans wore bronze plates for armor, attached to leather garments.

MYCENAEAN SHIELD
Mycenaeans carried shields made of leather over a wooden base. Most were shaped like an "8." Others were rectangular, and later ones were round.

MYCENAE
Mycenae was at the center of power in Greece in the late **Bronze Age**. The walls surrounding the city were up to 40 feet (12.5 m) high. Over the main entrance was a triangular piece of stone, carved with two lions.

CHARIOT WAR

Wealthy and noble Mycenaean warriors fought in light, two-wheeled war chariots pulled by a pair of horses. Two-person chariots carried a driver and a fighter armed with a spear or bow and arrow.

BATTLE REPORT

The Siege of Troy

In the *Iliad*, the ancient Greek poet Homer told the story of the great Mycenaean victory over the legendary city of Troy. In the tenth year of war, the attacking Mycenaeans finally got into the city by hiding inside a wooden horse. The Trojans pulled the horse and the hidden Mycenaeans inside their city walls. The Mycenaeans broke out of the wooden horse at night and opened Troy's city gates. They let in other Mycenaean warriors, and a bloodbath followed. Hundreds of Trojans were killed, and others were taken away as slaves.

ALL-POWERFUL HOPLITES

From about 800 BCE, a new kind of warrior became supreme in Greece—the **hoplite**. Hoplites were foot soldiers, or **infantry** men, who fought for their city state. Until around 350 BCE, they were all-powerful on the battlefield, even against chariots and **cavalry**.

MARCHING IN STEP
Greek hoplites would march into battle singing a war song, known as a paean. The rhythm helped them keep in step.

CITIZEN SOLDIERS

As most city states could not afford professional soldiers, the ordinary **citizens** had to do the fighting. They bought their own armor and weapons (costing perhaps a year's wages) and gave up time for training. For this, they wanted something in return. They asked for a say in how the city state was run. This may have been the beginning of democracy— government by the people.

EQUIPPED FOR VICTORY

Hoplites fought to defend their city, their families, and their possessions. To do this, they bought the best weapons and armor they could afford.

FIGHTING TALK

The toughest fighters in Greece

The Spartans valued military skills above all else. Their hoplites were the best in Greece. Hoplite selection began at birth—all infants were inspected, and any weak-looking babies were killed. This ensured that only the strongest survived. Male Spartans dedicated their lives to being soldiers. They were allowed to marry, but they could not live with their wives until after the age of 30.

HOPLITE TRAINING

Spartan boys began their military training at the age of seven. They were sent to military boarding schools, where discipline was tough. Athenians did not begin their official training until the age of 18. Before that, they kept fit with athletic games.

FISTICUFFS

Boxing was an important part of a hoplite's training. Boxers fought bare-fisted and without a break until one fighter gave up.

RACE-IN-ARMOR

As well as boxing, hoplite training activities included discus throwing, javelin throwing, and wrestling. The most famous training event was a running race called the "hoplitodromos." The naked competitors wore only a helmet and leg armor, and carried a shield. They ran two lengths of a straight track called the "stadion." This was around 380 yards (350 m).

TOUGHENING UP

Wrestling bouts were an excellent way of keeping young men ready for battle at short notice. But with no fixed rounds and few rules, the fighting was not for the faint-hearted.

FIGHTING TALK

A military life

At the age of 20, after 13 years of training, male Spartans served as full-time soldiers for 20 years. At the age of 40, they went into the **reserves** and could be called up to fight at any time until they were 60. The male citizens of Athens had just two years of hoplite training. They returned to their normal lives at the age of 20 but had to stay battle-ready until they were 60.

BATTLE ARMOR

By around 600 BCE, the hoplites of most city states were wearing roughly the same kind of armor. It consisted of a shield, helmet, hinged body armor, and upper and lower leg armor.

HELMET
This helmet has eye openings that are shaded by a leather visor.

CUIRASS
This hoplite's chest is protected by armor known as a cuirass.

ZOMA
A heavy leather belt offered additional protection for a hoplite's chest. Only the richest hoplites could have afforded a zoma such as this.

GREAVES
Hoplites wore leg armor called greaves. Greaves were fastened behind the leg with leather straps.

FIGHTING TALK

Body protection
The main protection for the back and front of a hoplite's body was a cuirass. The bronze "bell" cuirass weighed at least 15 pounds (7 kg). It swung open on a hinge. After around 500 BCE, hoplites began to wear much lighter cuirasses made of linen with bronze plates.

HARD HATS

Greek helmets were made of bronze and came in two basic styles. The earlier Kegel or Illyrian helmets fitted over the head but left the face clear. The later Corinthian helmet covered most of the face but left openings for the eyes, nose, and mouth. Both styles might have a showy crest on the top.

SHIELD

Hoplites used large shields to defend themselves. Shields were made of wood and bronze and were 3 feet (1 m) in diameter.

PLUMED HELMET

This hoplite's helmet has a crest made of horse hair. Crests made hoplites appear taller and more frightening.

LINEN ARMOR

Armor made of linen reinforced with metal plates was lighter and cheaper than all-metal armor.

WEAPONS OF WAR

A hoplite's most important weapon was his long spear, known as a **dory**. Hoplites used their spears to attack the enemy without getting too close. Hoplites also carried swords for hand-to-hand fighting.

SPEARHEAD FOR STABBING

A dory had a leaf-shaped spearhead made of iron. In battle, a hoplite pointed the spear forward and thrust the spearhead at the enemy.

SHAFT

A dory had a wooden shaft. The wood often came from ash trees. Ash is a very strong wood, which is also used to make tools.

SWORD

A hoplite often carried a sword called a *xiphos*. He used it in close combat or when his spear had broken.

BUTT-SPIKE

At the bottom of the spear was a sharp bronze spike, which could be stuck into the ground. It could also be used as a weapon if the spearhead had broken off.

POORER SOLDIERS

Not all fighting men could afford the gear of a hoplite. Poorer soldiers, or "peltasts," armed themselves with whatever they could lay their hands on. They often had light javelins for throwing at the enemy. The bow and arrow was also used. The cheapest weapons of all were wooden clubs and **slingshots** for throwing stones.

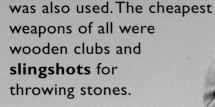

LIGHT INFANTRY
Groups of peltasts would throw javelins or stones, or fire arrows at the enemy army as it advanced.

COMBAT STATS

Dory and sword

- **Length of dory:** 8 feet 10 inches (2.7 m)
- **Weight of dory:** 2-4 pounds (1-2 kg)
- **Length of sword:** about 20 inches (50 cm)
- **Weight of sword:** about 17.6 ounces (500 g)

THE MIGHTY PHALANX

In battle, Greek hoplites took up a formation known as the phalanx. They formed a shield wall bristling with deadly spears. In attack or defense, the phalanx was master of the battlefield for hundreds of years.

BATTLE LINES

Hoplites operated in groups of 144, each divided into four units of 38. In battle, they lined up in rows, one behind the other. The number of rows depended on the width of the battlefield, the number of troops available, and the commander's battle plan. When a warrior in the front row fell, the man behind him stepped forward to take his place. In this way, the shield wall remained unbroken.

TIGHT FORMATION

The phalanx brought about dramatic changes in ancient Greek warfare. The tight-knit formation exploited the fact that horses will not charge at large solid objects. Suddenly, the nobleman's chariot, which had previously dominated on the battlefield, was useless.

READY TO CHARGE!

Enemy phalanxes would advance together and crash against each other on the battlefield. Soldiers in the front row used their spears to attack while the ones behind pushed forward with their shields. Retaining formation was essential for victory.

BATTLE REPORT

The Battle of Leuctra, 371 BCE

Greek armies usually put their most powerful forces on the right-hand side of the phalanx. In the famous Battle of Leuctra, the Theban commander Epaminondas broke this tradition. Facing the Spartans, he put a massive force of crack troops, 50 lines deep, on the left. The Thebans charged, smashed the Spartan right, and won the battle. The power of Sparta was broken for ever.

WARSHIPS

Much of Greece is surrounded by sea, so naval battles were not uncommon. Warships were used to ram and sink enemy vessels. The real advantage for the ancient Greeks came with the invention of the trireme, around 550 BCE.

SAIL POWER
Greek warships had sails so the wind helped to push them through the water. The sails were woven from linen or wool.

OARS
Early warships, such as this one, had a row of oarsmen on each side. However, triremes were fast battleships powered by three banks of oarsmen.

TACTICS AT SEA

Trireme captains wanted to sink the ships of their opponents, not board them. First, large catapults fired missiles to set enemy vessels on fire or damage their oars, sails, and **rigging**. After this, using the huge ram (pointed spike) in the **bow**, triremes tried to smash holes in an enemy's **stern** or side. Another tactic was to get alongside the enemy's ship and break its oars. This left it helpless.

TRIREME
This modern replica of an Athenian trireme shows the three sets of oars used to power through the water.

COMBAT STATS

Trireme

- **Shape and size:** shaped like a pencil, 121 feet (37 m) long, 16 feet (5 m) wide, 10 feet (3-10 m) deep (excluding the mast)
- **Construction:** made of wood—fir, pine, oak, and cedar, depending on what was available to the shipyard
- **Rowers:** 170 in three tiers on each side (108 could not see the sea)
- **Maximum speed:** 8-9 knots (10.5 mph or 17 km/h) but only for a short time because the rowers got tired

CITADELS AND SIEGES

The stone-walled cities of early Greece were almost impossible to capture. Attackers had to climb over the walls or try to burn down the gates. This began to change around 450 BCE, when siege engines—battering rams, catapults, and later, towers on wheels—started to appear.

UNDER SIEGE
The defenders have moved their front line outside the city's walls. This stops the enemy from getting close enough to use battering rams and other siege engines. The archers rain arrows on the attackers, while the spiked stakes defend against cavalry and chariots.

SIEGE TACTICS

The Greeks had three ways of dealing with an army shut behind high stone walls. One was to attack the villages and farms nearby. This forced the enemy to come out and protect its people and their property. Second, they could starve the citizens out by surrounding the city and cutting off its supplies. The third tactic was all-out attack.

BELLY BOW

The belly bow was a bolt-shooting catapult like a crossbow. The vicious weapon consisted of a springy steel bow, string of twisted animal gut, and a sturdy stand. It fired darts or "bolts" that could pierce through shields and the thickest armor.

BALLISTA

Greek **ballistas** fired deadly bolts using a massive bow and bowstring. Ballista bolts could smash a door, kill a horse, or go right through a man at 110 yards (100 m).

BATTLE REPORT

The Siege of Syracuse, 414–413 BCE

The Athenians' siege of the city of Syracuse in Sicily was one of the longest and most disastrous in ancient times. The city walls were protected by the sea, marshes, and steep rocks. The attackers tried to cut off supplies by building a wall of their own outside those of Syracuse. They also attacked with missile- and rock-throwing engines. All assaults failed, and Syracuse and its inhabitants survived. Athens never recovered from the shock and cost of this defeat.

WARS WITH PERSIA

The Greeks and **Persians** were at war between 492 and 449 BCE. The Persians invaded Greece twice. The Greeks eventually drove the invaders back on both occasions. However, the wars were hard-fought, and the second Persian attack began with a Greek defeat at Thermopylae.

THE BATTLE OF MARATHON, 490 BCE

The power of the Greek hoplites was shown at the famous Battle of Marathon. An army of 9,000 Athenian hoplites, with 1,000 allies from the city state of Plataea, charged 25,000 Persian invaders on the beach at Marathon. The lightly armed Persians were slaughtered. The amazing victory cost the lives of 192 Athenians and 11 Plataeans.

CHARGE!
With spears at the ready, Greek hoplites conduct a surprise attack on the Persian army on the beach at Marathon. The Greeks chose the moment carefully, when the enemy cavalry were not on the battlefield.

BATTLE REPORT

Battle of Thermopylae

In 480 BCE, the Greeks faced a second Persian invasion force in the narrow Pass of Thermopylae. Led by King Leonidas of Sparta, the Greeks were greatly outnumbered. They managed to hold back the huge invasion force for several days. A Greek traitor then showed the Persians a mountain path that led behind the Greek lines. From here, the Persians could attack the Greeks from the rear. When he realized what was happening, Leonidas dismissed most of his troops. To give them time to escape, 300 Spartans and 700 soldiers from Thespiae bravely fought on. In history's most famous "last stand," they held up the Persian army of around 100,000 until every Greek lay dead.

DYING LIKE A TRUE SPARTAN

King Leonidas, played by Gerard Butler in the 2003 movie *300*, wears the red cloak of Sparta just before his death at Thermopylae. In reality, as well as a red cloak, Leonidas would have worn a helmet, body armor, and a red tunic.

PERSIAN DEFEAT

In the summer of 480 BCE, after his victory at Thermopylae, Persia's King Xerxes took Athens. In the same year, the Athenians defeated the Persians in two great battles, one at sea and one on land. The second Persian invasion had been crushed.

BATTLE OF SALAMIS

Persia's huge fleet met Athenian warships in a narrow waterway called the Straits of Salamis. The close-packed Persian vessels, with hardly room to move, were smashed by a devastating Greek assault.

KING XERXES IN DEFEAT

Persia's King Xerxes watches in horror as his fleet is destroyed by Athenian triremes.

BATTLE OF PLATAEA, 479 BCE

King Xerxes of Persia went home when his fleet was sunk at Salamis (479 BCE). The Greeks then turned their attention to the 70,000 Persian soldiers who remained. Thinking their enemy had split up, the Persians made the big mistake of attacking. More than 38,000 Greek warriors came together and, led by the Spartans, Tegeans, and Athenians, won a stunning victory. The Persian invasions were over.

REVENGE!

At Plataea, the Spartans took their revenge for the death of King Leonidas at Thermopylae.

COMBAT STATS

Battle of Salamis, 480 BCE

- **Size of Greek fleet:** about 370 ships
- **Size of Persian fleet:** about 700 ships
- **Greek commander:** Themistocles
- **Persian commander:** King Xerxes
- **Naval losses:** Greece—40 ships; Persia—200 ships

ALEXANDER THE GREAT

The finest of all Greek warriors was Alexander of Macedonia (356–323 BCE). Known as Alexander the Great, he created a vast empire that stretched from Greece in the west to India in the east.

KING OF MACEDONIA

Alexander the Great led his army over 12,000 miles (19,000 km) to create the largest empire the world has ever seen.

BUCEPHALUS

King Alexander rode into battle on his favorite horse, Bucephalus. The noble stallion carried his master from Greece to India, through Egypt, Persia, and Afghanistan.

ALEXANDER'S ARMY

Alexander's army was the greatest military force of its time. As well as the traditional phalanx of hoplites, he used light and heavy cavalry, archers (some on horseback), and a new weapon—a 21-foot (7-m) spear known as the "sarissa."

SARISSA
The Macedonians replaced the dory with the longer sarissa as their hoplites' main weapon.

INFANTRY
The Macedonian infantry (known as Foot Companions) was organized into disciplined fighting units of 256 men.

ALEXANDER
Alexander the Great, played here by Colin Farrell in the 2004 movie *Alexander*, surveys his army before a battle.

BATTLE REPORT

Battle of the Hyardaspes River, 326 BCE

Alexander was a military genius who remained undefeated in battle. He won one of his finest and hardest victories in India, against King Porus. Porus' army of around 30,000 infantry and 3,000 cavalry was supported by over 100 war elephants. The 11,000 Greeks crossed a swollen river to attack the enemy on two sides. Their infantry disabled the elephants by slashing their hamstrings with axes.

GREECE VS. ROME

Alexander the Great's empire fell apart after his death. Soon, a new power was on the rise—Rome. Roman warriors entered Greece four times, finally conquering the whole region in 146 BCE. The warriors of ancient Greece had finally met their match.

THE MACEDONIAN WARS

About a hundred years after Alexander's death, Rome was at war with Carthage, a city in North Africa. King Philip of Macedonia sided with Carthage, so the Romans invaded his kingdom in 214 BCE. After three more wars (200–196 BCE, 192–188 BCE, and 150–148 BCE), all of Greece was overrun and became part of the mighty Roman Empire.

ROMAN LEGIONARY
By the second century BCE, Roman **legionaries** were fast replacing hoplites as the number one warrior of the Mediterranean region.

BATTLE REPORT

The Battle of Corinth, 146 BCE

The Romans took over Macedonia in 150–149 BCE. Annoyed, the other Greek states set up the anti-Roman Achaean League. Headed by the hugely rich Corinth, the league declared war on Rome. This was not a wise move. Outnumbered 2:1, the Greek phalanxes were overwhelmed by the Roman legionaries, and the city of Corinth was utterly destroyed.

ROMAN CONQUERERS

Like the Greeks, Roman soldiers were well disciplined and fought in tight formation. They used shields and spears in a similar way to the hoplites.

GLOSSARY

ballista a war machine for launching huge arrows at the enemy during a siege

bow the front section of a ship

bronze a type of metal made by mixing copper and tin

Bronze Age a time in the past, between about 3,000 and 4,000 years ago, when bronze was the toughest metal known

cavalry warriors who fight on horseback

citizen a free man living in a city state

city state a Greek city and the land around it

dory a long hoplite spear

empire a country or state and all the lands it controls outside its own

hoplite a heavily armed Greek foot soldier who was also a citizen

infantry warriors who fight on foot

legionary a Roman foot soldier

Peloponnesian relating to the large area of Greece southwest of Athens

Persians people from the country known as Iran today

phalanx a group of hoplites in close formation for battle

professional working in a particular occupation for pay

reserves soldiers outside the front line who were held back in case they were needed

rigging the ropes attached to the sails and mast of a ship

siege engine a large war machine used to attack a town or city

slingshot a catapult

stern the back section of a ship

tactics in battles, the carefully planned way in which forces are organized and used

trireme a Greek warship with a sail and three banks of oars on each side

FURTHER INFORMATION

Books

Alexander the Great: True Lives by Andrew Langley (Oxford University Press, USA, 2009)

Ancient Greece by Anne Pearson (DK Eyewitness Books, 2007)

Did Greek Soldiers Really Hide Inside the Trojan Horse?: And Other Questions about the Ancient World by Carol M. Scavella Burrell (Lerner Publications, 2010)

Greek Warrior by Deborah Murrell (W.B. Saunders Company, 2012)

Greek Warriors by Charlotte Guillain (Heinemann-Raintree, 2010)

Web Sites

Ancient Greek Warfare

www.historyforkids.org/learn/greeks/war/

A web site packed with information about Greek warfare and hoplites.

Ancient Military

www.ancientmilitary.com/greek-warriors.htm

An excellent research site for teachers with masses of detail.

The Battle of Marathon, 490 BCE

www.eyewitnesstohistory.com/marathon.htm

This useful site contains information about the Battle of Marathon.

The Peloponnesian Wars

www.history.com/topics/trojan-war/videos#the-peloponnesian-war

History is retold through music and art in this entertaining and informative video about key events of the Peloponnesian War.

Warriors of Ancient Greece

www.youtube.com/watch?v=ECFtQytko0g

This YouTube video is a tribute to Greek warriors as the defenders of Western civilization.

Index